A STRAIGHTFORWARD GUIDE TO BUYING AND SELLING A HOME IN BRITAIN AND FRANCE

Andrew Davies

Straightforward Publishing
www.Straightforwardco.co.uk

Straightforward Publishing
Brighton BN2 4EG

© Straightforward Publishing 2007

ISBN 184716 010 7
ISBN 13: 9781847160102

Printed by Biddles Ltd Kings Lynn Norfolk

Cover design by Bookworks Islington

Contents

Introduction

INTRODUCTION

The process of buying and selling a home is probably the single most important activity undertaken by individuals in their lifetime. The money and effort involved means that it is a process that must be carried out effectively and with a clear knowledge of the elements involved.

When buying or selling a home, particularly buying, you will liaise with a whole number of people, professional or otherwise: solicitors, estate agents, finance brokers, surveyors, banks and building societies and so on. All of these people play a vital role in the house purchase/sale transaction.

All of these parties involved will have many years experience of property and not all of them will be acting in your own best interests.

Very often, the person who owns the property or who wishes to purchase a property is the one with the least knowledge of the process and is the one who stands to lose the most. When initially looking for a property, wrong decisions are made. The price paid for a property is quite often too high, with disastrous consequences later on. The condition of the property may leave a lot to be desired. There are many stories of people losing out on this single most important transaction.

Unfortunately, it is a fact that if mistakes are made at the outset then you might spend the rest of your life recovering from the consequences.

Like all areas of life, knowledge is a precious asset and can help you make informed decisions. This book will go some way to assist you in being able to make informed decisions and to understand more about the processes involved in buying and selling a home.

In this brief guide, I begin by looking at general considerations when buying a property, as opposed to selling. Normally, people will look for the next home before selling their own home. This covers the all important areas of budgeting for the costs associated with purchasing a property, from raising the deposit to calculating the costs involved in the actual transaction, such as stamp duty, fees and the costs of removal.

Chapter 2 looks at all of the considerations involved in looking for a home and covers all aspects of the process of finding a home, from the area to the mechanisms for locating the ideal home and considerations to be taken into account when looking.

Chapter 3 looks at the role of the estate agent and what kind of service you can expect to receive if looking to buy or sell through an agent.

Chapter 4 looks at all the intermediaries involved from mortgage brokers to surveyors.

Chapter 5 looks more thoroughly at the process of buying and selling.

Chapter 6 looks more in depth at the range of mortgages on the market.

Chapter 7 looks at the process of conveyancing and will provide an insight into the process of conveying a property from one person to another.

Chapter 8 looks at the process of moving and all the associated costs and also provides useful contact information.

Chapter 9 takes a brief look at the mechanics of buying and selling in Scotland.

Finally, chapter 10 looks at buying a property overseas. There is a list of useful websites at the end of the book.

Frances James 2006.

1

GENERAL CONSIDERATIONS WHEN BUYING A HOUSE OR FLAT

This chapter looks generally at the processes involved in buying and selling a property. Each area is developed more fully in subsequent chapters.

Budget

Before beginning to look for a house you need to sit down and give careful thought to the costs involved in the whole process. The starting point is to identify the different areas in the overall transaction.

Deposit

Sometimes the estate agent will ask you for a small deposit when you make the offer (see Estate Agents, chapter 2). This indicates that you are serious about the offer and is a widespread and legitimate practice, as long as the deposit is not too much, £100 is usual.

The main deposit for the property, i.e., the difference between the mortgage and what has been accepted for the property, isn't paid until the exchange of contracts. Once you have exchanged contracts on a property the purchase is legally binding. Until then, you are free to withdraw. The deposit cannot be reclaimed after exchange.

Banks will normally lend up to 95% of the purchase price of the property. However, the less you borrow, the more favourable terms you can normally get from bank or building society.

Stamp duty

Stamp duty is a tax paid on a property over £60,000. The duty is 1% of purchase price between £60.000 and £250,000, 3% between £250,000 and £500,000 and 4% over £500,000 which adds a significant amount to the conveyancing costs. If the house or flat costs £60,000 or under no duty is payable.

Other costs

A solicitor normally carries out conveyancing of property. However, it is perfectly normal for individuals to do their own conveyancing. All the necessary paperwork can be obtained from legal stationers and it is executed on a step-by-step basis.

It has to be said that solicitors are now very competitive with their charges and, for the sake of between £200-£300, it is better to let someone else do the work which allows you to concentrate on other things.

Land Registry

The Land Registry records all purchases of land in England and Wales and is open to the public (inspection of records, called a property search)

The registered title to any particular piece of land or property will carry with it a description and include the name of owner, mortgage, rights over other persons land and any other rights. There is a small charge for inspection. A lot of solicitors have direct links and can carry out searches very quickly. Not all properties are registered although it is now a duty to register all transactions. (see chapter 7, conveyancing)

Searches

These are checks with the local authority and other bodies which ascertain whether or not there are any proposed developments or other works in the vicinity of the property which could jeopardise the value of the property in the future or the well being of the occupants.

There is normally a pro forma used for this as the questions are standard, and a charge of between £80-200 will be incurred.

Structural surveys

The basic structural survey is the homebuyers survey and valuation which is normally carried out by the building society or other lender.

This will cost you between £100-150 and is not really an in-depth survey, merely allowing the lender to see whether they should lend or not, and how much they should lend. Sometimes, lenders keep what they refer to as a retention, which means that they will not forward the full value (less deposit) until certain defined works have been carried out.

If you want to go further than a homebuyers report then you will have to instruct a firm of surveyors who have several survey types, depending on how far you want to go and how much you want to spend.

A word of caution. Many people go rushing headlong into buying a flat or house. They are usually exhilarated and wish to complete their purchase fairly quickly in order to establish their new home. If you stop and think about this, it is complete folly and can prove very expensive later. A house or flat is a commodity, like other commodities, except that it is usually a lot more expensive. A lot can be wrong with the commodity that you have purchased which is not immediately obvious. Only after you have completed the deal and paid over the odds for your purchase do you begin to regret what you have done.

The true price, of a property is not what the estate agent is asking, certainly not what the seller is asking. The true market price is the difference between what a property similar to the one in good condition is being sold at and your property minus cost of works to bring it up to that value.

Therefore, if you have any doubts whatsoever, and if you can afford it anyway, get a detailed survey of the property you are proposing to buy and get the works required costed out. When negotiating, this survey is an essential tool in order to arrive at an accurate and fair price. Do not rest faith in others, particularly when you alone stand to lose.

One further word of caution. As stated, a lot of problems with property cannot be seen. A structural survey will highlight those. In some cases it may not be wise to proceed at all.

Mortgage fees

Mortgage indemnity insurance. This is a one-off payment if you are arranging a mortgage over 70-80% of lenders valuation. This represents insurance taken out by the lender in case the purchaser defaults on payments, in which case the lender will sell the property to reclaim the loan. It is to protect the mortgage lender not the buyer.

The cost of the insurance varies depending on how much you borrow. A 90% mortgage on a £60,000 property will cost between £300-600. For a 100% mortgage it is usually much higher. You have to ask yourself, if you are paying up to £2,000 for this kind of insurance on a 100% mortgage, is it not better to try to raise the money to put down a bigger deposit. Always think about the relative economics. A lot of money is made by a lot of people in house buying and selling. The loser is usually the buyer or seller, not the host of middlemen. So think carefully about what you are doing.

Mortgage arrangement fees

Depending upon the type of mortgage you are considering you may have to pay an arrangement fee. You should budget for up to £300.

Removals

Unless you are not moving far and are considering doing it yourself, budget for hiring a removal firm. This will depend on how many possessions you have and how much time and money you have. Take care when choosing the removal firm. Choose one who comes recommended if possible.

There are other costs too. Reconnection of telephone lines and possibly a deposit, carpets, curtains and plumbing-in washing machines. How much you pay will probably depend on how handy you are yourself.

There are also smaller incidental costs such as redirecting mail by the post office. We will be discussing moving home in more depth later on in chapter 8.

The table below will give you an idea of typical costs, such as solicitors fees, stamp duty, land registry fees and search fees when buying a property. The costs are based on a purchase of a typical London property. Other costs as discussed above will be extra.

House price	Solicitors fees (av)	Stamp duty	Land Registry	Search fees	Total fees
£150,000	650	1,500	150	235	2,535
£200,000	684	2,000	150	235	3,069
£300,000	757	9,000	220	235	10,212
£500,000	898	15,000	220	235	16,353
£750,000	1069	30,000	420	235	31,724
£1m	1372	40,000	420	235	42,027
£1.5m	1895	60,000	700	235	62,830
£2m	2208	80,000	700	235	83,143
£2.5m	2723	100,000	700	235	103,658
£3m	3656	120,000	700	235	124,591
£3.5m	4231	140,000	700	235	145,166
£4m	4871	160,000	700	235	165,806

Now turn to the Key Points from Chapter One overleaf.

Key Points From Chapter One.

- Give careful thought to all the costs of buying and selling property.

- Banks will normally lend up to 95% of the purchase price of a property. The more that you lend the more that it costs.

- If the house or flat costs over £60,000, stamp duty will be payable.

- You should consider very carefully the need for a full structural survey when buying a property.

- Always bargain, never offer the asking price.

2

LOOKING FOR A HOME

Obviously, where you choose to buy your house will be your own decision. However, it may be your first time and you may be at a loss as to where to buy, i.e. rural areas or urban areas, the type and cost of property or whether a house or flat. There are several considerations here:

Area

Buying in a built up area has its advantages and disadvantages. There are normally more close communities, because of the sheer density. However, it is true to say that some built up areas have become fragmented by population movement, "Yuppification" etc. Local services are closer to hand and there is a greater variety of housing for sale. Transport links are also usually quite good and there are normally plenty of shops.

Disadvantages are less space, less privacy, more local activity, noise and pollution, less street parking, more expensive insurance and different schooling to rural environments. The incidence of crime and vandalism and levels of overall stress are higher in built up, more urban areas. This is not the case with all built up areas. It is up to the buyer to carry out research before making a commitment.

If you are considering buying in a rural area, you might want to consider the following: there is more detached housing with land, more space and privacy. However, this can be undermined by the "village" syndrome where everyone knows your business, or wants to know your business. There is also cleaner air and insurance premiums can be lower. Disadvantages can be isolation, loneliness, lower level of services generally, and a limited choice of local education.

Choosing your property

You should think carefully when considering purchasing a larger property. You may encounter higher costs, which may include:

- Larger, more expensive, carpeting

- More furniture. It is highly unlikely that your existing furniture will suit a new larger home.

- Larger gardens to tend. Although this may have been one of the attractions, large gardens are time consuming, expensive and hard work.

- Bigger bills

- More decorating

- Higher overall maintenance costs

Purchasing a flat

There are some important points to remember when purchasing a flat. These are common points that are overlooked.

Maintenance charge. If you purchase a flat in a block, the costs of maintenance of the flat will be your own. However, the costs of maintaining the common parts will be down to the landlord (usually) paid for by you through a service charge. There has been an awful lot of trouble with service charges, trouble between landlord and leaseholder. It has to be said that many landlords see service charges as a way of making profit over and above other income, such as ground rent, which is usually negligible after sale of a lease.

Many landlords will own the companies that carry out the work and retain the profit made by these companies. They will charge leaseholders excessively for works which are often not needed. The 1996 Housing Act attempts to strengthen the hand of leaseholders against unscrupulous landlords by making it very difficult indeed for landlords to take legal action for forfeiture (repossession) of a lease without first giving the leaseholder a chance to challenge the service charges.

Be very careful if you are considering buying a flat in a block – you should establish levels of service charges and look at accounts. Try to elicit information from other leaseholders. It could be that there is a leaseholders organisation, formed to manage their own service charges. This will give you direct control over contracts such as gardening, cleaning, maintenance contacts and cyclical decoration contracts. Better value for money is obtained in this way. In this case, at least you know that the levels will be fair, as no one leaseholder stands to profit.

Leasehold Reform Act 1993 as amended by the Commonhold and Leasehold Reform Act 2002

Under this Act, all leaseholders have the right to extend the length of their lease by a term of 90 years. For example, if your lease has 80 years left to run you can extend it to 170 Years. There is a procedure in the above Act for valuation. Leaseholders can collectively also purchase the freehold of the block. There is a procedure for doing this in the Act although it is often time consuming and can be expensive. There are advantages however, particularly when leaseholders are not satisfied with management.

Viewing properties

Before you start house hunting, draw up a list of characteristics you will need from your new home, such as the number of bedrooms, size of kitchen, garage and study and garden. Take the estate agents details with you when viewing. Also, take a tape measure with you.

Assess the location of the property. Look at all the aspects and the surroundings. Give some thought as to the impact this will have in your future life.

Assess the building. Check the facing aspect of the property, i.e., north, south etc. Check the exterior carefully. Earlier, I talked about the need to be very careful when assessing a property. When you have made your mind up, a survey is essential.

Look for a damp proof course - normally about 15cm from the ground. Look for damp inside and out. Items like leaking rainwater pipes should be noted, as they can be a cause of damp. Look carefully at the windows. Are they rotten? Do they need replacing and so on. Look for any cracks. These should most certainly be investigated. A crack can be symptomatic of something worse or it can merely be surface. If you are not in a position to make this judgement then others should make it for you.

Heating is important. If the house or flat has central heating you will need to know when it was last tested. Gas central heating should be tested at least once a year.

All in all you need to remember that you cannot see everything in a house, particularly on the first visit. A great deal may be being concealed from you. In addition, your own knowledge of property may be slim. A second opinion is a must.

Buying an old house

If you are considering purchasing a modern house and making improvements then there are a number of things to think about:

Consider whether your proposed alterations will be in keeping with the age and style of the house, and neighbouring houses, particularly in a terrace. A classic mistake is that of replacing doors and windows with unsympathetic modern products. Again, salesmen will sell you anything and quite often won't provide the correct advice;

If appropriate, you should consider contacting the Victorian Society or the Georgian Group for advice on preserving your home. Both offer leaflets to help you carry out appropriate restoration. It is often a good idea to employ an architect or surveyor to oversee any alterations you are considering. For local contractors contact the Royal Institute of British Architects or Royal Institute of Chartered surveyors.

Renovation grants

These may be available from local authorities, although there are stringent requirements. They are means tested and the higher your income the more you are expected to pay. For further details you should contact your local authority direct.

Disabled facilities grant

A grant may be available to adapt a property for a disabled person, for example improving access into and around the home and adapting existing facilities within it. These grants are mandatory, but a discretionary grant is available to make a property suitable for the accommodation, welfare or employment of a disabled person. A Department of Environment leaflet, Help for Disabled People with Adaptation and Other works provides basic information.

Planning permission

If you are considering alterations of a significant nature, either internal or external, you may need planning permission from your local authority. You may need planning permission if you plan to change the look or external aspect of the building or if you are intending to change the use.

You are allowed to carry out some work without planning permission, so it is worth contacting the local authority. You should also ask about building regulations. These are concerned with the materials and methods of building adopted. Regulations for work carried out in conservation areas are strict. The building control department at your local authority will be able to advise you about building regulations.

28

Buying a listed building

Buildings of architectural or historical interest are listed by the Secretary of State for National Heritage following consultation with English Heritage, to protect them against inappropriate alteration. In Wales, buildings are listed by the Secretary of State for Wales in consultation with CADW (Heritage Wales). In Scotland, they are listed by the Secretary of State for Scotland, in consultation with Historic Scotland.

If you intend to carry out work to a listed building, you are likely to need listed building consent for any internal or external work, in addition to planning permission. The conservation officer in the local planning department can provide further information.

Buildings in conservation areas

Local authorities can designate areas of special architectural or historical significance. Conservation areas are protected to ensure that their character or interest is retained. Whole towns or villages may be conservation areas or simply one particular street.

Strict regulations are laid down for conservation areas. Protection includes all buildings and all types of trees that are larger than 7cm across at 1.5m above the ground. There may be limitations for putting up signs, outbuilding or items such as satellite dishes. Any developments in the area usually have to meet strict criteria, such as the use of traditional or local materials.

This also applies to property in national parks, designated Areas of outstanding natural Beauty and the Norfolk or Suffolk Broads.

Whether or not a property is listed or is deemed to be in a conservation area will show up when your conveyancer carries out the local authority search.

Buying a new house

There are a number of benefits to buying a new house. You have the advantages of being the first occupants. There should not be a demand for too much maintenance or DIY jobs, as the building is new.

There will however be a defects period which usually runs for 6 months for building and 12 months for electrical mechanical. During this period you should expect minor problems, such as cracking of walls, plumbing etc, which will be the responsibility of the builder.

Energy loss will be minimal. A new house today uses 50 per cent less energy than a house built 15 years ago; consider the savings over an older property. An energy rating indicates how energy efficient a house is. The National House Building Council uses a rating scheme based on the National Energy Services Scheme, in which houses are giving a rating between 0 and 10. A house rated 10 will be very energy efficient and have very low running costs for its size.

Security and safety are built in to new houses, smoke alarms are standard and security locks on doors and windows are usually included.

When the house market is slow developers usually offer incentives to buyers, such as cashback, payment of deposit etc. Sometimes they offer a part exchange scheme. These are definitely worth looking into. However, with part exchange you may not get the price you were looking for.

Building Guarantees

All new houses should be built to certain standards and qualify for one of the building industry guarantees. These building guarantees are normally essential for you to obtain a mortgage and they also make the property attractive to purchasers when you move. A typical Guarantee is the National Housebuilding Council Guarantee (NHBC).

Websites for housebuilders

Most developers have their own websites with details and picture of their developments. These include both new properties and

refurbished. In addition there are several websites that specialise in new properties only. Two such sites are:

www.freeagents.co.uk
www.newhomesnetwork.co.uk

Buying a Rented House

Right to Buy

If you rent your house from your council, a new town, a housing association or housing association trust, you will probably be able to buy it at a discount.

In order to buy:

- You must have a secure tenancy

- You must have spent at least two years as a tenant of your current landlord or another right to buy landlord

- The house or flat must be a separate dwelling and your only or principle home.

The discount will vary according to length of tenancy and type of property. For further details you should contact your landlord. A new scheme, called Statutory Purchase Grant, is now available to assist those tenants of public sector landlords without the right to buy to purchase their homes. The discount is not so generous as the right to buy, usually ranging from £10,000-£13,000. Again details should be obtained from your landlord

Shared ownership property

There are properties available on a shared ownership basis, usually from housing associations. Local Authorities also provide such schemes, although rarely.
The main principle is that you buy a percentage of the property, say 50% and you rent the rest, with a service charge if a flat. As time goes by you can "staircase up" to 100% ownership. This is a scheme specially designed for those who cannot meet the full cost of outright purchase in the first instance. Usually, your total monthly outgoings are smaller than they would be if you purchased outright.

Another similar scheme, run by certain housing associations is called "Do it Yourself Shared ownership', where you find a house or flat and the housing association will purchase, and you then purchase a share in it, much the same as shared ownership.

For further details you should contact a large housing association in your area who will point you in the right direction.

Self-build property

Self-build is another option for obtaining a new home. However, it is time consuming and not for the faint hearted. You need to be organised and to have organised the finances and your work programme. Usually the biggest problem is finding a suitable plot of land.

There is a lot of competition. It also means that you will, unless you employ an agent, be charged with supervising a number of skilled craftsmen. Self-build usually works out cheaper than buying off a developer but it is certainly not an easy option. For more information and advice check out the following websites:

www.homebuilding.co.uk

This is run by the publishers of homebuilding and renovation magazine which is the leading magazine for homebuilders. The site is magazine style with lots of articles and also a link to www.plotfinder.net. This is a recently established database of land for sale and houses to renovate. There is an annual subscription cost, currently £35.

www.buildstore.co.uk
This site is owned by a group of venture capitalists, individuals and companies involved in the self build market. Again, there

is a mix of articles and also adverts plus a site similar to plotfinder.

www.ebuild.co.uk

This site is published by specialist publisher's webguides on line. The site includes a directory of suppliers from architectural salvage to waste disposal with links to useful sites.

www.npbs.co.uk

This is the site of Norwich and Peterborough Building Society, who offer mortgages for self build projects. The loan for self-build is released in stages linked to the building of the property.

Now read the Key Points from Chapter 2 Overleaf.

Key Points From Chapter Two

- When looking for a house, consider essential points such as area and services.

- Think carefully about costs involved and also work if you are considering buying a larger property.

- When purchasing a flat, consider maintenance charges.

- Before viewing, draw up a list of characteristics you will need from a house or flat.

- There are a number of advantages to buying a new house, such as new construction and minimal energy loss.

- Other schemes available include self-build housing

3

THE ROLE OF ESTATE AGENTS IN BUYING AND SELLING PROPERTY

Estate Agents

What to expect from an estate agent:

- Advice on the selling or asking price of a house or flat - they know the local market

- Advice on the best way to sell (or buy) and where to advertise; they should discuss an advertising budget with you

- If selling a meeting to visit, assess and value your home and also to take down the particulars of your home. The Property Misdescriptions Act, which arose out of the bad old days of the 1980's, prevents agents from using ambiguous statements to enhance the sale of the property. You should look at the points carefully as people who are disappointed after reading such a glowing report will not purchase.

- They may ask for details of recent bills, such as council tax and electricity. They should also be willing to give advice on fixtures and fittings included in the sale.

- They should be willing to show potential buyers around your home if you are not available.

- Don't expect to have to pay for a for-sale board although some lenders will try to make a charge.

Choosing an agent if selling

Consider the following points:
- They ought to sell your type of property or specialise in one particular area of the market

- They should be a member of one of the professional bodies such as the National Association of Estate Agents, the Royal Institution of Chartered Surveyors, The Incorporated Society of Valuers and Auctioneers, The Architects and Surveyors Institute or the Association of Building Engineers.

- Obtain quotes of fees, including the basic charge and any extras you might have to pay for, such as advertising in specialist publications.

Choose at least two agents to value the house, if instructing an agent.

Selling through one or more agents Sole agency.
Offering an agent sole agency may reduce the fee. This can be done for a limited time. After this you can instruct multiple agents. With sole agency you can sell privately.

Joint sole agents
With this arrangement, two or more agents co-operate in the house sale and split the commission. The agents may charge a higher commission in this case.

Multiple agency

This means that you have several agents trying to sell your home, but only pay the agent who sells your property.

Buying property using the internet

There are a number of websites that also detail properties, some are independent and some are owned by the large players. The following are a selection of the main sites:

www.rightmove.co.uk.

This is one of the largest sites, jointly owned and run by Halifax, Royal Sun Alliance, Connell and Countryside assured Group. They jointly claim to represent more than 170,000 properties covering 99% of UK postcodes. The main function of this site is as a property search site, enabling people to search for property by name of area and postcode.

Each property has a reference number and will have a photo and details. These can be obtained by clicking on the property. There is much useful information, including room sizes.

www.fish4.co.uk

This site is owned by a consortium of local newspapers groups and came into being in 1999. They claim that there is over 174,000 properties for sale and rent and it is updated daily.
Fish is, basically, online advertising, with sections covering many activities, including property.

www.assertahome.co.uk

This is owned by the Commercial Union and Norwich Union Insurance Groups. The claims of the website are that it can help the buyer to find a property, move home and settle in. There are links to the Insurance Broker, John Charcoal.

www.propertyfinder.co.uk

This site began life in 1995 and is connected to several prominent estate agency groups.

www.primelocation.co.uk

This site was launched in 2000 by a consortium of estate agents. This site deals with more expensive properties.

Selling property using the internet

Although estate agents are still the main avenues for selling property, as we have seen, the web is beginning to play a more significant part. In addition to the websites detailed, almost all agents now have their own website. This is really an electronic shop window where your property is displayed. Buyers interested in your property should be able to e-mail the estate agent directly for a viewing.

Now read the key points from chapter 3.

Key points from chapter 3

- Estate agents have a number of roles. However, the main function is to guide the buyer/seller through the process from beginning to end.

- Make sure that you choose the appropriate agent if selling. Make sure that the agent is a member of a professional body.

- You will need to consider whether you wish to sell through more than on estate agent.

- There are a number of websites dealing with buying and selling property. This is often a cheaper way of purchasing or selling.

4

DEALING WITH INTERMEDIARIES

When you buy a house or flat there is always someone in the middle, be it estate agents, moneylenders or solicitors.

Getting a mortgage

There are various forms of buy-to-let mortgages and lenders should be willing to discuss all the available options with you. The lender, after taking details, will give you a mortgage certificate saying how much they are willing to offer. This is not a definite offer but shows the other parties that you are a serious buyer.

The following can offer mortgages:

- Building societies. The usual choice.

- Banks.

- Insurance companies. Life insurance is needed for endowment mortgages. Insurance companies may also offer mortgages linked to their insurance policies.

- Builders and property developers. As an incentive to buy, builders or developers may offer to arrange your mortgage for you. They are often able to get good deals with low interest rates for the start of the mortgage, but rates may increase rapidly in the long term. Check that the developer is reputable.

Independent financial advisors

These advisers will do the work for you. However, a word of caution. Independent advisers are in the business of selling product and getting commission. That does not always mean the best deal for you. In the past, independent advisers have had bad press, particularly over pensions. It is best to ask the adviser leading questions about the product, particularly if they are selling you an endowment mortgage. For example, how much do you pay before your money starts working for you. The adviser's fee has to be covered then there are the administration charges. More about mortgages in chapter

Conveyancers

This is the legal process of buying a house. You can choose a licensed conveyancer or a solicitor. There is a lot of competition so look around. Always ask for a written estimate which covers all cost, including disbursements which are the costs associated with stamp duty, searches and registration with the land registry etc.

The conveyancer's main tasks are to purchase your property, which will begin as soon as you have put in your offer and it has been accepted. They will:

- Make local authority and other searches

- Check the seller's right to sell and that there are no complications such as sitting tenants, undisclosed mortgages, alterations that did not have planning permission or disputes over boundaries and land ownership.

- Examine the details at the land registry or details about the history of the property going back at least 15 years if the house is unregistered.

- Find out about any shared driveways or drains, you're right to access and any public rights to access.

- check boundaries and who is responsible for their upkeep.

- Check guarantees for any previous work such as damp treatment or building work.

- Sometimes arrange surveys and a valuation report.

If buying a new house;

- Check that the house is built correctly, that all services have been laid on and that responsibility for maintenance of services such as drainage and sewerage has been handed over to the local authority.

- Check who has responsibility for the access roads.

- Confirm any restrictions imposed by the developer, such as future alterations, cutting down of trees or parking restrictions.

Prior to exchange of contracts
- Examine the draft contracts, ensuring that all points are included.

- Exchange contracts with the sellers conveyancer.

- Receive the deposit.

- Arrange signature of mortgage documentation before or after contracts have been exchanged.

After completion

- notify the lender and insurance companies of the completion.

- Arrange payment of the stamp duty.

- Register you as owner with the land registry along with details of your lender. He may require you as well as the seller to sign the transfer documents. Pass the deeds on to the lender.

- Send you a statement confirming that everything has been completed and any money due to you.

The conveyancers main tasks during the sale

- Liase with the buyer's conveyancers.

- Ensure that mortgages, and any other financial arrangements such as hire purchase, and outstanding service charges, are cleared on completion.
- draw up a draft contract and package including a copy of the title deeds or entry at the land registry. Deeds will need to be obtained from your lender.

- If the property is not registered with the land registry details about the property, from the title deeds, over at least 15 years, need to be prepared.

- Receive the deposit on behalf of the seller. If it is stated in the contract that the conveyancer is to act as "agent for the vendor" the payment will be passed on for the seller to put towards the purchase.

Transaction protocol

This is a scheme introduced by the law society to streamline the buying and selling process for England and Wales. The seller's solicitor decides whether or not to use it. If he does so then he will put together an information pack for the buyer's solicitor. This includes the property registration details, a standard list of fixtures and fittings and details of who is responsible for maintaining different property borders.

The Home Charter Scheme (Northern Ireland)

The Home Charter scheme was set up for solicitors in Northern Ireland. It sets standards of service when solicitors help you buy or sell a property. When looking for a solicitor look for one who is registered as a home chartered solicitor.

Using surveyors

Surveyors are involved either on behalf of the lender or on behalf of yourself, depending on who instructs them. They carry out a number of different reports, from a valuation report to a full in depth survey.

The largest professional association is the Royal Institute of Chartered Surveyors (RICS). Members of the Incorporated

Society of Valuers and Auctioneers (ISVA) also carry out home surveys.

Whilst the basic home buyers survey will cover the general condition of the property and any structural defects likely to affect the value of the property, along with value and reinstatement for insurance purposes, the Building Structural Survey is rather more in depth and covers the following:

Full Structure

In Depth Analysis of property as a whole
Roof space
Under floors
Services including drainage, wiring and central heating.

The inspection generally takes several hours and will provide a full report plus costings. As I mentioned earlier, it sometimes pays dividends to invest in this initial survey, especially as a bargaining tool.

Home search relocation agents

If you are moving to a distant region and regular visits to carry out inspection of properties are not practical then you can employ a relocation agent to carry out the initial house hunting for you. They take account of all your requirements and even negotiate price for you. The Association of Relocation Agents produces a directory of agents which is free. The cost of using a relocation agent is about 1.25 % of the purchase price. There may also be a registration fee.

Now read the key points from chapter 4

Key Points From Chapter Four

- Take great care when choosing a mortgage.

- If dealing with independent financial advisers, get as much information about the product offered as possible.

- Choose only a licensed Conveyancer.

- Choose your estate agent carefully, check credentials.

5

BUYING AND SELLING

The process of buying a property

Although we have discussed the basic steps in selling a property, and outlined the basic costs, it is useful to outline a few more areas connected with the purchase of a property.

The first step is to find the property you want. This is a long and sometimes dispiriting process. Trudging around estate agents, sorting through mountains of literature, dealing with mountains of estate agents details, scouring the papers and walking the streets! However, most of us find the property we want at the end of the day. It is then that we can put in our offer.

One useful way of determining the respective values of property in different areas is to visit a website set up for that purpose, www.hometrack.co.uk. This particular site collects price information from selected estate agents in different postcode areas across the country. At the time of writing, prices are currently available for London and the southeast, the southwest, Birmingham and the Midlands and the north of England. Before you decide to look, a little research into prices and comparisons with what you can afford might be useful.

Making an offer
You should put your offer in to the estate agent or direct to the seller, depending who you are buying from.

As discussed earlier, your offer should be based on sound judgement, on what the property is worth not on your desire to secure the property at any cost. A survey will help you to arrive at a schedule of works and cost. If you cannot afford to employ a surveyor from a high street firm then you should try to enlist other help.

In addition, you should take a long and careful look at the house yourself, not just a cursory glance. Look at everything and try to get an idea of the likely cost to you of rectifying defects. However, I cannot stress enough the importance of getting a detailed survey.

Eventually, you will be in a position to make an offer for the property. You should base this offer on sound judgement and you should provide a rationalisation for your offer, if it is considerably lower than the asking price. You should make it clear that your offer is subject to contract and survey (if you require further examination or wish to carry out a survey after the offer).

Putting your own home on the market

Most people moving try to secure the sale of their own home before looking for a new one. If you haven't started to sell your house yet, you are advised to do so as soon as possible.

You need also to arrange finance. A lot of people have had the nightmarish experience of stepping into an estate agents and being besieged by "independent" financial advisors wishing to sell you their product. Be very careful at this stage. See "getting your mortgage" chapter 5.

Exchange of contracts

Once the buyer and seller are happy with all the details stated in the contract and your conveyancer can confirm that there are no outstanding legal queries, those conveyancing will exchange contracts. The sale is now legally binding for both parties. You should arrange the necessary insurances, buildings and contents from this moment on as you are now responsible for the property.

Buying with a friend

The 1996 Family Law Act brought in the concept of cohabiting couples having the same rights as married couples. This will apply particularly if your marriage starts to break up and you wish to ascertain property rights.

However, it is wise to draw up a cohabitation contract prior to purchase which will put in writing how the property is shared and will make clear the situation after break-up.

The cohabitation contract can include any conditions you wish and is drawn up usually by a solicitor. There are standard forms for cohabitation agreements which can include financial arrangements stating who pays for the mortgage, who can call for a sale, mutual wills, and who pays for and owns possessions.

You can obtain a leaflet concerning this from a Citizens Advice Bureau or from a solicitor.

Completing a sale

This is the final day of the sale and normally takes place around ten days after Exchange. Exchange and completion can take place on the same day if necessary but this is unusual. On day of completion, you are entitled to vacant possession and will receive the keys. See chapter seven for more details on the conveyancing process.

Buying a property in an auction

Property can be purchased in an auction. A small amount are sold in this way. Usually properties sold at auction are either unusual or difficult to put a price on or are repossessions. Auction lists can be obtained from larger estate agents or are advertised in papers. The Estates Gazette, published by the Royal Institute of Chartered Surveyors give details of auctions in each publication. Normally, this magazine is available to subscribers only although it can be ordered through a newsagent.

Preparing for auction

Because the auction is the final step of the sale, you should have any conveyancing carried out and your mortgage arranged. You will probably need to sell your old home. With this in mind it is a quick way of finding a property if you need to move quite quickly. However, it is likely that your choice of property may be limited and you will need to work on it. Many properties at auction are sub- standard, this is why they are there in the first place.

- Ask for the package compiled by the auctioneer. It will include full details of the property and the memorandum of agreement which is equivalent to the contract.

- View the house

- Organise a conveyancer and instruct him to carry out searches and arrange surveys
- If you like the property, set yourself a price limit to bid to, and arrange a mortgage.

Buying before auction

If the sales details quote "unless previously sold" the seller may be prepared to accept offers before the auction, but he will still accept a fast sale and you will be signing an auction contract. You will need to arrange conveyancing and finance very quickly.

If you are buying at the auction itself, you should remember that the fall of the hammer on your bid is equivalent to the exchange of contracts as for a private sale. You have made a legal arrangement and you will be expected to pay 10-15% deposit on the spot with the remainder of the payment within 28 days.

At the auction

If you are doubtful about your own ability then you can appoint a professional to act on your behalf although they will obviously charge for their services.

The seller may be selling subject to a reserve price. If this is the case, it is normally stated in the particulars. The actual figure is not usually disclosed but if the auctioneer states something like "I am going to sell this property today" it is an indication that the reserve price has been reached.

Sale by tender
As an alternative to auction, sale by tender is like a blind auction; you don't know what the other potential buyers are

offering. A form of tender is included in the sales details and sometimes sets out the contract details. Always check these details with your conveyancer, because often you cannot pull out after the offer is accepted.

Buyers put their offers in an envelope, sometimes with a 10% deposit. These must be received by the seller's agent at a specified date, at which time the seller will accept one of the offers.

Sale by tender is sometimes used when there have been two or three offers at similar prices.

House swapping

House swapping is an unorthodox but cost effective way of obtaining the property that you are looking for. It is a very efficient way of buying a property. Essentially, you find the property that you want and the seller moves into your house. There is no chain because you are cutting out other buyers. Obviously, the biggest problem is finding someone that you want to swap with and who wants to swap with you.

In practice, the estate agent should be the ideal key player in any swap arrangement. They have a large number of people on their books and who have provided details of their requirements. However, this way of operating seems to be beyond all but the most enterprising estate agencies. In practice, most swaps happen through coincidence.

Saving money through swapping homes

There is a significant saving to be made by swapping homes. If you are the one trading down, for example you have a home worth £275,000 and you want to swap it for a flat worth

£150,000, the owner of the flat will be paying for your house with part cash part property. As far as the revenue is concerned this is not a sale on which you would pay stamp duty, but a transfer on which you would pay a notional sum of just £5. However, in this particular type of transaction solicitors must draw up the deal as a single contract with the more expensive property paid partly in kind and partly in cash. You can also save on estate agents fees if you find your swap independently.

A useful website dealing with home swaps is:
www.webswappers.com

This site deals with anything that can be swapped but has an increasing number of properties. Registration on the site is free.

Selling your home
Estate agents

Ask for quotes from at least three agents before instructing one or more of them. The fee is normally based on the selling price of the house and is between 1 - 3 per cent of the final selling price. However, VAT will be added on to this.

DIY Selling

If you want to save the cost of instructing an agent to sell your house, you could try to sell it yourself. Around 4 - 5% of homes in the UK are sold privately. There are a number of useful guides which are dedicated to this subject.

Setting the price
You need to see how much similar properties are sold for in the area. If this proves difficult, get a professional valuation.

See Yellow Pages under Surveyors or Valuers or contact the Royal Institution of Chartered Surveyors.

A valuation report will only value and will not assess structural soundness. A survey is needed for that.

Put together the sales particulars in the same way that an estate agent would. It is advisable to put a disclaimer on these details such as "these particulars are believed to be accurate and are set out as a general outline only for the guidance of interested buyers. They do not constitute, nor constitute parts of, an offer or contract.

There are a number of ways you can advertise your property. Local papers will advertise for you and also there are papers such as LOOT (free ads paper, covering most regions) In addition, there are a number of companies with a computerised sales network who will charge you a flat fee for advertising. Be accurate with the details - you may leave yourself open to damages through misrepresentation. If an offer is made to you then you should then hand matters over to your solicitor.

As discussed, some sellers handle their own conveyancing lock stock and barrel. This includes the legal side. However, this book cannot advise you on legal conveyancing. That is a separate matter. Suffice to say that it follows a standard format. It is easier, in the light of the reduced prices available to appoint a solicitor to do this side for you.

Selling by auction

Selling by auction can be a fast way to sell your house so you should ideally have made provision for new accommodation and storage for furniture if necessary. A date for completion is set before the auction, usually four weeks after. This is included in the selling guide. Properties are usually sold by auction in order to obtain the highest market price. An auction is also a good method if it is otherwise difficult to put a value on a property, for example if the property is unusual, as the market finds the best price.

The cost of selling by auction

Auctioneers fees are along the lines of those charged by estate agents - in the region of 1-3 per cent, but on top of this you will have to pay the preparation costs. The auctioneer will prepare a brochure and probably special advertising which you will be expected to pay for. A solicitor will be needed to carry out the legal work for you.

You should remember that you will have to pay auction costs even if the property does not sell.

The aim of the auction is obviously to exceed the asking price but if you do not even reach the reserve price you can still sell privately to an interested party, possibly immediately after the auction.

If the auction is successful the auctioneer signs the contract on your behalf and receives the 10% deposit. the remaining balance is usually required within 28 days, but this detail should be specified in the contract drawn up beforehand.

Earlier we saw a table giving typical costs of buying a house in London. The table below gives typical costs of the sale of a property.

Typical costs of buying a property

House price	Solicitors fees	Estate agents fees	Total fees
£150,000	620	2,436	3,056
£200,000	652	3,276	3,928
£300,000	722	4,954	5,676
£500,000	852	8,052	8,904
£750,000	1,004	11,987	12,991
£1m	1,312	15,714	17,026
£1.5m	1,804	23,503	25,307
£2m	2,143	31,042	33,185
£2.5m	2,578	38,816	41,394
£3m	3,502	46,627	50,129
£3.5m	4,088	54,097	58,185
£4m	4,675	60,604	65,279

Now read the key Points from Chapter five overleaf.

Key Points Chapter 5

- The aim, when selling your property and buying another, is to organise the process so that the seller moves into his new home when the buyer moves into his.

- Make an offer on what you think the property is worth and not the asking price.

- Look over the property you wish to buy very carefully indeed.

- If purchasing jointly, draw up a cohabitation contract.

- If you are buying in an auction take great care.

6

MORTGAGES

Most people purchasing a property will need a mortgage. There are many products on the market and deposits are not always required. However, it is crucial that you are in possession of all the facts when making a decision about a mortgage.

Financial advisers will give you plenty of advice but not always the best advice. Sometimes it is better to go to the lender direct. Before you talk to lenders, work out what your priorities are, such as tax advantage, investment potential, early repayment and so on. Make sure that you are aware of the costs of life cover.

Lenders-Banks and building societies

There is little or no difference between the mortgages offered by banks and building societies. Because banks borrow against the wholesale money markets, the interest rate they charge to borrowers will fluctuate (unless fixed) as and when their base rate changes. Building societies however, which will rely more heavily on their savers deposits to fund their lending, may adjust the interest rate charged for variable mortgages only once a year. This may be a benefit or disadvantage, depending on whether rates are going up or down.

Centralised lenders

Centralised lenders borrow from the money markets to fund their lending and have no need for the branch network operated by banks and building societies. Centralised lenders, which came to the fore during the 1980s, particularly the house price boom, have been criticised for being quick to implement increases but slow to implement decreases, through rate reductions. This is, simply, because they exist to make profit. Therefore, you should be cautious indeed before embarking on a mortgage with lenders of this kind.

Brokers and "independent" financial advisors

Brokers act as intermediaries between potential borrowers and mortgage providers. If they are "tied" agents they can only advise on the products of one bank, insurance company or building society. If they are independent they should, technically, advise and recommend on every product in the market place.

A word of warning. It is up to you to ask detailed questions about any product a broker offers you. You should ask if they will receive a fee or commission, or both for any sale they arrange for you. Many brokers sell unsuitable products because they receive healthy commissions. In the 1980s it became impossible to enter an estate agents without being forced to enter into discussions with financial advisers who were intent on selling you products which made them a lot of money. If possible, you should arrange a mortgage direct with a bank and avoid so called independent brokers.

How much can you borrow

There is a standard calculation for working out the maximum mortgage that you will be allowed. For one borrower, three times annual salary, for a joint mortgage, two or two and a half times combined. Lenders, however, will vary and some will lend more. Be very careful not to overstretch yourself.

Deposits

Most banks and building societies lend 95% maximum. Some lend 100% but will usually charge a premium for doing so. Lenders dealing with buy-to-let mortgages will usually ask for a minimum of 15% deposit. Some lenders are prepared to lend 90% but you pay a premium for the privilege of doing so. The more that you put down the better deal that you are likely to get from the lender.

Joint mortgages

If you want a joint mortgage, as for any other shared loan you and your partner have a shared responsibility for ensuring that the necessary repayments are made. If something happens to one partner then the other has total responsibility for the loan.

Main types of mortgage

Endowment

With this type of mortgage, you have to take out an endowment insurance policy which is then used to pay off the mortgage loan in a lump sum at the end of the term. There are a number of different types designed to achieve the same end:

- Low cost with profits. This is the usual sort of endowment, guaranteeing to pay back part of the loan only. However, because bonuses are likely to be added, it is usually enough to pay off the loan in full;

- Unit linked endowment. With this, the monthly premiums are used to buy units in investment funds. The drawback is that there is no guarantee how much the policy will be worth on maturity, since this depends on how well the investments have performed.

A word of warning. Endowment products are pushed heavily by financial brokers. There was an obsession with them in the 1980's. This is because they earn big commission for those people that sell them. Like all good salespeople, advisers failed to reveal the down sides.

These are:

Endowments are investment linked and there is no guarantee that they will have matured sufficiently at the end of the term to repay the mortgage. This leaves you in a mess. A repayment mortgage will definitely have paid off the mortgage at the end of the term.

If you change your mortgage and decide that you do not wish to continue with an endowment mortgage, and so cash in the policy early you will almost certainly get a poor return unless it is close to maturity. In the early years of the policy, most of your payments will go towards administration and commission (a fact that your broker does not always reveal) The alternative in these circumstances is to maintain the endowment until it matures, treating it as a stand alone investment which will, hopefully, make you some money eventually.

Repayment mortgages

This mortgage, where the borrower makes regular repayments to pay the mortgage off over the term is a fairly safe bet. However, if you plan to move house every five years then this will not necessarily be the best mortgage for you. With a repayment mortgage, you pay interest every month but only a small proportion of the capital, particularly in the early years of the mortgage. An endowment mortgage, while more risky, could be better for you under these circumstances, since you can transfer the plan from property to property, while it can, hopefully, grow steadily as it matures.

Pension mortgages

Similar to the other products except that the payments go into a personal pension plan with the remainder after paying the mortgage forming the basis of a pension. The same characteristics apply as to the others.

Interest only mortgage

The borrower pays interest only on the loan, and decides how he or she will pay the loan off at the end. The lender will want to know this too.

Mixed mortgages

A new development is that one or two lenders now allow borrowers to mix a combination of mortgages in one deal, customising the mortgage to suit each individual.

Foreign currency mortgages

Some foreign banks offer short-term mortgages in the foreign currency of that bank. Their lending criteria can be much more relaxed than trying to borrow from a British lender. The advantage of this sort of mortgage depends on currency fluctuations. If the pound is stable or rises, the borrower benefits. If the pound drops, the borrower will have to pay more. These types of home loans should be left to more sophisticated investors as there is the potential to get into trouble unless you have a clear grasp on the implications of such a mortgage.

Cashbacks

You have probably seen the adverts offering large sums of cashback if you take a particular product. If you read the small print, unless you take the highest mortgage available with the highest deposit then you will not get anywhere near such a sum. You should remember that money given with one hand is money taken back with another. If you decide to take up such a mortgage, then see what you will get back and see what the terms are, i.e., interest rates and so on.

What to do if you feel that you have been given wrong advice

The mortgage lending market is very complicated and many people have suffered at the hands of financial advisors and others who have given incorrect advice. Mortgage regulation has not been very tight. However, the basic framework is as follows:

- Sales of mortgage linked investments like endowments or pensions are regulated by the Financial Services Authority. Anyone selling investments must be qualified and registered and must be able to clearly demonstrate that the policy that they have recommended is suitable. All registered individuals and firms are inspected by regulators and can be fined or expelled from the industry if guilty of wrongly selling products.

- By contrast, information on mortgages is currently regulated by the industry only, voluntarily, under a code of mortgage practice sponsored by the Council of Mortgage Lenders. Although most of the big players are signed up to the code there are still some who are not. Check first before taking advice.

How to complain

- Complain first to the company that sold you the product, going through its internal complaints procedure.

- If you are unhappy with the firm's decision, approach the relevant complaints body. For mortgage advisors employed directly by lenders, or complaints about lenders generally, contact the financial Ombudsman service on 020 7694 1000 or www.financial-ombudsman.org.uk

- For mortgage lenders which are not building societies or banks but which are signed up to the mortgage code, the Chartered Institute of Arbitrators 020 7421 7444 www.arbitrators.org will assist.

- If your complaint is about a mortgage broker, contact the Chartered Institute of Arbitrators which may be able to help if the firm is registered under the code.
- Complaints about endowments, pensions and other investments is handled by the Financial Services Authority 020 7676 1000

www.fsa.gov.org and dealt with by the financial ombudsman Service.

The most common complaint is to do with endowments. A lot of people bought products which they came to regret. They are a major source of profit to the provider-and all those in between-but the person left holding the problem is the consumer.

If you believe that you have been given bad advice about anything to do with the insurance or investment side of a product then you can approach the following organisations:

- The Company that sold you the product;

- The Personal Investment Authority (PIA) which is an organisation responsible for regulating lenders and individuals who give advice on and sell insurance and investment products;

- The PIA Ombudsman who can investigate any firm registered with PIA.

You can also write to:

- Securities and Investment Board, which supervises PIA.

- Insurance Ombudsman, which is a government appointed consumer watchdog, which investigates complaints from individuals, and decides who is right or wrong.

- Investment ombudsman, if your problem is to do with investment products.

The Building Society Association or the British Bankers Association have free publications that should help you. In addition, the Consumers Association, "Which" runs regular articles on mortgages.

Remember - always ask questions. Never rush into anything. Always take advice if you are uncertain. The 1980s were a repeat of every other house price boom in the era and gave rise to many unscrupulous operators with their own interests at heart, not yours. There is nothing new here, people usually fall for old tricks dressed up in new names.

Banks and building societies themselves are usual a better source, a safer source than individual advisers.

Borrowing and the internet

Almost all lenders have their own sites and many operate internet only loans with keener rates than those available on the high street. But there are also growing numbers of mortgage broker sites, offering mortgage calculators so that you can work out how much you can afford to borrow and how much the true cost of your loan will be. The following are a selection of independent sites:

www.moneysupermarket.co.uk
This is an online mortgage broker with a choice of over 4000 variable, fixed rate, capped and discounted mortgages as well as more specialist loans for right to buy, buy to let and self build property, also self certification loans.

www.moneynet.co.uk

This is an independent on line mortgage broker, offering mortgages from over 100 lenders. Again, as with all these sites it will provide a clear and comprehensive picture of mortgages available and is easy to use, just follow the instructions.

www.moneyextra.co.uk
An independent financial advisor with access to over 4500 products including all kinds of mortgages for all types of client.

Now read the Key Points from Chapter six overleaf.

Key Points From Chapter Six

- There are many mortgage products on the market. Choose carefully. Understand advice- make sure all is clear.

- The more you borrow, the more you pay at the outset and over the term.

- If you are given wrong advice or feel aggrieved in any way there are mechanisms for complaint.

7
CONVEYANCING A PROPERTY

Conveyancing, or the practice of conveyancing, is about how to transfer the ownership of land and property from one person or organisation to another. Land and property can include freehold property, leasehold property (residential) or can include business leases. *Essentially, the process of conveyancing lays down clear procedures for the conveyancer and also sets out each party's position during the sale or acquisition.*

Before understanding the process of conveyancing, however, it is essential to understand something about the legal forms of ownership of property.

Legal ownership of property

There are two main forms of legal ownership of property in Great Britain. If you are about to embark on the sale or acquisition of a house or flat (or business) then you will be dealing in the main with either freehold or leasehold property.

It is very rare indeed to find other forms of ownership, although the government is about to introduce a form of ownership called 'common hold' that will, in essence, create the freehold ownership of flats, with common responsibility for communal areas. At the time of writing, this bill is being passed through Parliament.

Freehold property

In general, if you own the freehold of a house or a piece of land, then you will be the outright owner with no fixed period of time and no one else to answer to (with the exception of statutory authorities).

There may be registered restrictions on title, which we will be discussing later. The property will probably be subject to a mortgage so the only other overriding interest will be that of the bank or the building society. The responsibility for repairs and maintenance and general upkeep will be the freeholders. The law can intervene if certain standards are not maintained.

The deed to your house will be known as the "freehold transfer document" which will contain any rights and obligations. Usually, the transfer document will list any "encumbrances" (restrictions) on the use of the land, such as rights of way of other parties, sales restrictions etc.

The deeds to your home are the most important documentation. As we will see later, without deeds and historical data, such as the root of title, it can be rather complicated selling property. This is why the system of land registration in use in this country has greatly simplified property transactions.

Any person owning freehold property is free to create another interest in land, such as a lease or a weekly or monthly tenancy, subject to any restrictions the transfer may contain.

Leasehold property

If a person lives in a property owned by someone else and has an agreement for a period of time, usually a long period, over 21 years and up to 99 years or 125 years, in some cases 999 years, then they are a leaseholder.

The conveyancing of leasehold property is, potentially, far more problematic than freehold property, particularly when the flat is in a block with a number of units.

The lease is a contract between landlord and tenant which lays down the rights and obligations of both parties and should be read thoroughly by both the leaseholder and, in particular, the conveyancer. Once signed then the purchaser is bound by all the clauses in the contract.

It is worth taking a little time looking at the nature of a lease before discussing the rather more complex process of conveyancing. Again, it has to be stated that it is of the utmost importance that both the purchaser and the vendor understand the nature of a lease.

The lease

Preamble

The start of a lease is called the preamble. This defines the landlord and purchaser and also the nature of the property in question (the demise). It will also detail the remaining period of the lease.

Leaseholders covenants

Covenants are best understood as obligations and responsibilities. Leaseholder's covenants are therefore a list of things that leaseholders should do, such as pay their service charges and keep the interior of the dwelling in good repair and not to, for example, alter the structure. The landlord's covenants will set out the obligations of the landlord, which is usually to maintain the structure and exterior of the block, light common parts etc.

One unifying theme of all leasehold property is that, notwithstanding the landlord's responsibilities, it is the leaseholder who will pay for everything out of a service charge.

75

Leases will make detailed provisions for the setting, managing and charging of service charges, which should include a section on accounting. All landlords of leaseholders are accountable under the Landlord and Tenant Act 1985, as amended by the 1987 Act. These Acts will regulate the way a landlord treats a leaseholder in the charging and accounting of service charges.

In addition, the 1996 Housing Act, as amended by the 2002 Commonhold and Leasehold reform Act has provided further legislation protecting leaseholders by introducing the right of leaseholders to go to Leasehold Valuation Tribunals if they are unhappy with levels and management of charges and also to carry out audits of charges.

It is vital that, when buying a leasehold property that you read the lease. Leases tend to be different from each other and nothing can be assumed. When you buy a property, ensure that the person selling has paid all debts and has contributed to some form of "sinking fund" whereby provision has been built up for major repairs in the future. Make sure that you will not be landed with big bills after moving in and that, if you are, there is money to deal with them. After a lease has been signed then there is little or no recourse to recoup any money owed. These are all the finer points of leases and the conveyancer has to be very vigilant. In particular read the schedules to the lease as these sometimes contain rather more detail.

One of the main differences between leasehold and freehold property is that the lease is a long tenancy agreement which contains provisions which give the landlord rather a lot of power to manage (or mismanage) and it is always a possibility that a leaseholder can be forced to give up his or her home in the event of non compliance with the terms of the lease. This is known as forfeiture.

Under legislation referred to earlier, a new 'no fault right to manage' has been introduced. This enables leaseholders who are unhappy with the management of their property, to take over the management with relative ease. The Act applies to most landlords, with the exception of Local Authorities.

These powers go a long way to curb the excesses or inefficiencies of numerous landlords and provide more control and greater security for leaseholders.

Check points

There are key areas of a lease that should be checked when purchasing. Some have already been discussed.

- What is the term left on the lease?

- Is the preamble clear, i.e. is the area which details landlord, tenant and demised (sold) premises, clear?

- Is the lease assignable- i.e. can you pass on the lease without landlords permission or does it need surrendering at sale or a license to assign?

- What is the ground rent and how frequently will you pay it?

- What is the level of service charge, if any, and how is it collected, apportioned, managed and accounted for?

- What are the general restrictions in the lease, can you have pets for example, can you park cars, do you have a designated space?

- What are the respective repairing obligations? As we have seen, the leaseholder will pay anyway but the landlord and leaseholder will hold respective responsibilities. This is an important point because occasionally, there is no stated responsibility for upkeep and the environment deteriorates as a consequence, diminishing the value of the property.

Two systems of conveyancing

After gaining an understanding of the nature of the interest in land that you are buying, it is absolutely essential to understand the two systems of conveyancing property in existence, as this will determine, not so much the procedure because the initial basic steps in conveyancing, such as carrying out searches, are common to both forms of land, registered and unregistered, but the way you go about the process and the final registration.

Registered and unregistered land

In England and Wales the method of conveyancing to be used in each particular transaction very much depends on whether the land is *registered* or *unregistered* land. If the title, or proof of ownership, of land and property has been registered under the Land Registration Acts 1925-86 then the Land Registry (see below) will be able to furnish the would-be conveyancer with such documentation as is required to establish ownership, third party rights etc. If the land has not been registered then proof of ownership of the land in question must be traced through the title deeds.

Registered land
As more and more conveyancing is falling within the remit of the Land Registry, because it is compulsory to register land throughout England and Wales, it is worth outlining this system briefly at this stage.
The Land Registration Acts of 1925 established the Land Registry (HM Land Registry). The Land Registry is a

department of the Civil Service, at its head is the Chief Land Registrar. All applications to the Land Registry must be made within the district in question.

There is a specific terminology in use within conveyancing, particularly within the land registry:

a) *a piece of land*, or parcel of land is known as a *registered title*
b) the owner of land is referred to as the *registered proprietor*
c) a conveyance of registered land is called *a transfer*
d) a transaction involving registered land is known as *a dealing*

The main difference between the two types of conveyancing *registered* and *unregistered* concerns what is known *as proof of title*. In the case of land that is unregistered the owner will prove title by showing the would-be purchaser the documentary evidence which shows how he or she came to own the land and property.

In the case of registered land the owner has to show simply that he or she is registered at the Land Registry as the registered proprietor. Proof of registration is proof of ownership, which is unequivocal. In registered land the documents proving ownership are replaced by the fact of registration. Each separate title or ownership of land has a title number, which the Land Registry uses to trace ownership, or confirm ownership.

The description of each title on the register is identified by the *title number,* described by reference to the filed plan (indicating limits and extent of ownership). With registered conveyancing the Land Registry keeps the register of title and file plan and title. The owner (proprietor) is issued with a Land Certificate. If the land in question is subject to a mortgage then the mortgagee is issued with a Land Certificate.

Production of the Land Certificate

With registered land, whenever there is a sale, or disposition, then the Land Certificate must be produced to the Land Registry in the appropriate district. If proved that a Certificate is lost or destroyed then a new one can be issued by the Land Registry.

The key steps in the process of conveyancing property

Before the buyer exchanges contracts on a property, whether registered or unregistered, and then completes the purchase a number of searches are always carried out. These are:

Enquiry's before contract
Local land charges search
Enquiry's of the local authority
Index map search

These are the most essential and common searches.

Making enquiry's before contract

These are enquiry's to the seller, or the Vendor of the property and are aimed at revealing certain facts about the property that the seller has no legal obligation to disclose to the buyer. There are certain matters, which are always raised. These are:

a) Whether there are any existing boundary disputes
b) What services are supplied to the property, whether electricity, gas or other
c) Any easements or covenants in the lease. These are stipulations in the lease, which give other certain rights, such as rights of way.
d) Any guarantees in existence
e) Planning considerations
f) Adverse rights affecting the property

g) Any fixtures and fittings
h) Whether there has been any breach of restriction affecting the property

If the property is newly built, information will be required concerning any outstanding works or future guarantees of remedying defects. Where a property is leasehold, information will be required about the lessor.

Registered conveyancers will use a standard form to raise these enquiry's, so that the initial search is exhaustive. As part of the move towards openness in the process of buying and selling property, and also an attempt to speed up the process of sale, the Law Society has introduced new forms which the solicitor, or buyer if carrying out his or her own conveyancing, is being encouraged to use. These are Seller's Property Information Forms relating to freehold and leasehold property, that the seller and solicitor will respectively fill in, a form relating to fixtures, fittings and contents and a form relating to complete information and requisitions on title.

These forms can be obtained from a legal stationers, such as Oyez and have the pre-fix Prop 1-7. See appendix 5 for examples of these forms.

If a conveyancer is being used then it is advisable to ask to whether or not they are using these newly introduced forms. The main point is that you should think long and hard about the type of questions that should be raised. The vendor does not have to answer the questions, but beware a vendor who refuses to disclose answers.

Answers given by the vendor do not form part of the subsequent contract and therefore cannot be used against that person in the event of future problems. However, the

Misrepresentations Act of 1976 could be evoked if a deliberate misrepresentation has caused problems.

Local land charges search

The Local Land Charges Act 1975 requires District Councils, London Borough Councils and the City of London Corporation to maintain a Local Land Charges Registry for the area. Local land charges can be divided into two areas:

a) Financial charges on the land for work carried out by the local authority
b) restrictions on the use of land

The register is further divided into twelve parts:

a) general financial charges
b) specific financial charges
c) planning charges
d) miscellaneous charges and provisions
e) charges for improvements of ways over fenland
f) land compensation charges
g) new town charges
h) civil aviation charges
i) open cast coal mining charges
j) listed buildings charges
k) light obstruction notices
l) drainage scheme charges

All charges are enforceable by the local authority except g and i, which are enforced by statutory bodies and private individuals generally.

A buyer should search in all parts of this particular register and this can be done by a personal or official search. A personal search, as the name suggests, involves the individual or their agent attending at the local authority office and, on paying the relevant fee, personally searching the register. The charges are registered against the land concerned and not against the owner. The official search is the one most favored because, in the event of missing a vital piece of information the chances of compensation are far higher than with a personal search.

With the official search a requisition for a search and for an official certificate of search is sent to the Registrar of Local Land Charges for the area within which the land is situated. There is a fee and the search is carried out by the Registrars staff, which results in a certificate being sent to the person making the request, which clearly outlines any charges.

The Registrar may require a plan of the land as well as the postal address. Separate searches are made of each parcel of land being purchased.

Local authority searches
There is a standard form in use for these particular types of searches. This is known as "Con 29 England and Wales" Revised April 2000, (see appendix) with the format of the form differing slightly for inner London boroughs. Any of the forms in the process can be obtained from legal stationers such as OYEZ, head office in The Strand London.

The standard forms in use contain a statement to the effect that the local authority is not responsible for errors unless negligence is proved. Many of the enquiry's relate specifically to planning matters, whilst other elements of the search are concerned about roads and whether they are adopted and whether there are likely to be any costs falling onto property owners.

We will be considering planning matters concerning the individual property a little later. Other enquiry's relate to possible construction of new roads which may affect the property, the location of sewers and pipes and whether the property is in an area of compulsory registration of title, a smoke control area or slum clearance area.

The form used is so constructed that part 2 of the form contains questions, which must be initialled by the purchaser before they are answered. Again these questions cover planning and other matters. Other enquiry's can be asked by the individual, which are answered at the authorities discretion.

In addition to the above, which are the major searches, there are others that the conveyancer has to be aware of. These are as follows:

Searches in the Index map and parcels index of the Land register

If the land has been registered the title will be disclosed and whether it is registered leasehold or freehold. Registered rent charges are also disclosed by the search. (See chapter 7.)

Commons Registration Act (1965) search

This act imposes a duty on County Councils to keep a register relating to village greens and common land and interests over them, such as right of way.

Coal mining search

The request for this search if relevant, is designed to reveal the whereabouts of mineshafts and should be sent to the local Area Coal Board office, or its equivalent. The search will disclose past workings and any subsidence, proposed future workings and the proximity of opencast workings. It is usually well known if there is a problem, or potential problem with coal mining in an area and this search is essential if that is the case.

Other enquiry's

There are a number of other bodies from which it might be appropriate to request a search. These include British Rail, Statutory undertakers such as electricity and gas boards, planning authorities generally, rent assessment committees and so on. These will only usually be necessary if there is a direct link between the property being purchased and a particular circumstance within an area or property.

Planning matters relating to specific properties

It is obviously very necessary to determine whether or not any illegal alterations have been carried out to the property you wish to purchase, before reaching the point of exchange of contracts. This is to ensure that the vendor has complied with relevant planning legislation, if any material changes have been made, and that you will not be required at a later date to carry out remedial work. The Local Authority maintains a register of planning applications relating to properties within their boundaries. In addition, the register will also reveal any planning enforcement notices in force against a particular property.

Questions such as these, and also any questions relating to the effect of Structure or local plans, (specific plans relating to local and borough wide plans for the future) should be made in writing to the local authority or an individual search can be carried out. Usually they are carried out if there is any suspicion that planning regulations may have been breached.

In addition, there may be other considerations, such as whether the building is listed or whether tree preservation orders relating to trees within the cartilage of the property are in force. It is certainly essential to know about these.

It is highly recommended that all of these searches are carried out and completed before contracts are exchanged.

The contract for sale

As with many other transactions, a sale of land is effected through a contract. However, a contract, which deals with the sale of land, is governed by the requirements of the Law of Property (miscellaneous provisions) Act 1989, the equitable doctrine of specific performance and the duty of the vendor to provide title to the property.

The Law of Property Act (Miscellaneous provisions) 1988 provides that contracts dealing with the sale of land after 26th September 1989 must be in writing. The contract must contain all the terms and agreements to which the respective parties to the transaction have agreed. The provisions of the Act do not apply to sales at a public auction, contracts to grant a short lease and contracts regulated under the Financial Services Act 1986.

If the person purchasing is doing so through an agent then the agent must have authority to act on behalf of the purchaser. Examples of agents are auctioneers and solicitors, also estate agents.

If the phrase "subject to contract" is used in a sale then the intention of both parties to the contract is that neither are contractually bound until a formal contract has been agreed by the parties, signed and exchanged. Therefore, the words "subject to contract" are a protective device, although it is not good to depend on the use of these words throughout a transaction

Procedures in the formation of contract

The vendor's solicitor will usually draw up an initial contract of sale. This is because only this person has access to all the necessary initial documents to begin to effect a contract. The draft contract is prepared in two parts and sent to the purchaser's solicitor (if using a solicitor); the other side will approve or amend the contract as necessary. Both sides must agree to any proposed amendments.

After agreement has been reached, the vendor's solicitor will retain one copy of the contract and send the other copy to the solicitor or person acting for the other side. The next stage is for the vendors solicitor to engross (sign and formalise) the contract in two parts. Both parts are then sent to the purchaser's solicitor or other agent who checks that they are correct then sends one part back to the vendor's solicitor.

Signing the contract

The vendors solicitor will obtain the vendors signature to the contract, when he is satisfied that the vendor can sell what he is purporting to do through the contract. The purchaser's solicitor or agent will do the same, having checked the replies to all enquiry's before contract. It is also essential to check that a mortgage offer has been made and accepted.

Exchanging contracts
Neither party to the sale is legally bound until there has been an exchange of contracts. At one time, a face to face exchange

would have taken place. However, with the rapid increases in property transactions this rarely happen nowadays. Exchange by post is more common. The purchaser will post his or her part of the contract together with the appropriate cheque to cover the agreed deposit, to the purchaser's solicitor or person acting on behalf of that Person. The purchaser's solicitor will usually insert the agreed completion date. On receiving this part of the contract the vendor will add his or her part and send this off in exchange. At this stage, both parties become bound under the contract.

A contract to convey or create an estate in land is registrable as a class C (IV) land charge, an estate contract. You should take further advice on this, as it is not current practice to do so.

The Contents of a contract

A contract will be in two parts, *the particulars of sale* and the *conditions of sale*. The particulars of sale give a physical description of the land and also of the interest, which is being sold. A property must be described accurately and a plan may be attached to the contract to emphasize or illustrate what is in the contract. The particulars will also outline whether the property is freehold or leasehold and what kind of lease the vendor is assigning, i.e., head lease (where vendor is owner of the freehold) or underlease, where the vendor is not.

It is very important to determine what kind of lease it is that is being assigned, indeed whether it is assignable or whether permission is needed from the landlord and it is recommended that a solicitor handle this transaction. This is because any purchaser of a lease can find his or her interest jeopardized by the nature of the lease. Where a sub-lease, or under lease is being purchased, the purchasers interest can be forfeited by the actions of the head lessee, the actions of this person being out of control of the purchaser.

Rights, such as easements and also restrictive covenants, which are for the benefit of the land, should be expressly referred to in the particulars of sale. In addition, the vendor should refer to any latent defects affecting his or her property, if known. This includes any encumbrances, which may affect the property.

Misdescription

If the property in the particulars of sale is described wrongly, i.e. there is a mis-statement of fact, such as describing leasehold as freehold land, calling an under-lease a lease or leaving out something that misleads the buyer, in other words, if the misdescription is material, then the purchaser is entitled to rescind the contract. Essentially the contract must describe what is being sold and if it does not, and the buyer is mislead then the contract is inaccurate. If the misdescription is immaterial and insubstantial, and there has been no misrepresentation then the purchaser cannot rescind the contract. However, if the misdescription has affected the purchase price of the property then the purchaser can insist on a reduction in the asking price. The purchaser should claim this compensation before completion takes place. The vendor has no right to rescind the contract if the misdescription is in the purchaser's favour, for example, the area of land sold is greater than that intended. Neither can the vendor compel the purchaser to pay an increased purchase price

Misrepresentation

Misrepresentation is an untrue statement of fact made by one party or his or her agent, which induces the other party to enter into the contract. An opinion and a statement of intention must be distinguished from a statement of fact. There are three types of misrepresentation, fraudulent misrepresentation, negligent misrepresentation and innocent misrepresentation. Fraudulent misrepresentation is a false statement made knowingly or without belief in its truth, or recklessly. The innocent party may sue through the tort of negligence either before or after the contract is complete and rescind the contract. Negligent misrepresentation, although not fraudulent, is where the vendor or his or her agents cannot prove that the statement they made in relation to the contract was correct. Remedies available are damages or rescission of the contract. Innocent misrepresentation is where the statement made was neither fraudulently or negligently but is still an untrue statement. Rescission is available for this particular type of misrepresentation. Rescission of contract generally is available under the Misrepresentation Act 1967 s 2(2).

Non-disclosure

Generally, in the law of contract, there is the principle of "caveat emptor" "let the buyer beware". In other words, it is up to the purchaser to ensure that what he or she is buying is worth the money paid for it. Earlier we talked about the importance of searches and also, particularly, the importance of the structural survey. Although the vendor has some responsibility to reveal any defects in the property it is always very advisable for the purchaser to ensure that all checks prior to purchase are carried out thoroughly.

Conditions of sale

There are two types of conditions, special conditions and general conditions. Special conditions are those which are specific to an individual contract, such as when a specific day is fixed for completion. The general conditions are those which have general application.

General conditions of sale are standard and are contained in the appendix to this book, "National protocol for domestic leasehold and freehold property." This is a complete guide to conveyancing in itself and can be obtained from the Law Society.

The general conditions of sale oblige the vendor to supply the purchaser with abstracts or any copies of a lease or agreement in writing. The vendor must always supply the purchaser with details of any tenancy agreements in existence. A deposit for the purchase will only be payable if there is a special or general condition to this effect, such a term is not implied into a contract. Under standard conditions a deposit of 10% of the purchase price is paid to the vendors solicitor prior to purchase but this can be varied between parties. The deposit should be in cash or by banker's draft at the date of the contract (exchange). Failure to pay, or payment by a cheque, which is subsequently dishonoured, is a breach and can lead to the vendor rescinding the contract. The general conditions specifically refer to this.

If there is any interest due, or expected on purchase money this will be dealt with in the special conditions of contract.

Completion

The requirements concerning completion are detailed thoroughly in the general conditions of sale. Payment on completion is one such detail. Payment on completion should be by one of the following methods:

a) legal tender;
b) bankers draft;
c) an unconditional authority to release any deposit by the stakeholder
d) any other method agreed with the vendor.

At common law, completion takes place whenever the vendor wishes and payment is to be made by legal tender.

Also dealt with in the general conditions is failure to complete and notices to complete. Failure to complete can cause difficulty for one of the other parties and the aggrieved party can serve notice on the other to complete by a specific date. The notice has the effect of making "time of the essence" which means that a specific date is attached to completion, after which the contract is discharged.

Return of pre contract deposits

The vendor must return any deposit paid to the purchaser if the purchaser drops out before the exchange of contracts. This cannot be prevented and was the subject of a House of Lords ruling.

The position of the parties after exchange of contracts

Once a contract has been exchanged the purchaser is the beneficial owner of the property, with the vendor owning the property on trust for the purchaser. The vendor is entitled to any rents or other profits from the land during this period, has the right to retain the property until final payments have been made and has a lien (charge/right) over the property in respect of any unpaid purchase monies.

The vendor is bound to take reasonable care of the property and should not let the property fall into disrepair or other damages to be caused during the period between exchange and completion. If completion does not take place at the allotted

92

time and the fault is the purchasers then interest can be charged on the money due.

The purchaser, as beneficial owner of the property is entitled to any increase in the value of the land and buildings but not profits arising. The purchaser has a right of lien over the property, the same as the vendor, in respect of any part of the purchase price paid prior to completion.

Bankruptcy of the vendor

In the unfortunate event of the vendor going bankrupt in between exchange and completion, the normal principles of bankruptcy apply so that the trustee in bankruptcy steps in to the vendor's shoes. The purchaser can be compelled to complete the sale. The trustee in bankruptcy is obliged to complete the sale if the purchaser tenders the purchase money on the completion day.

Bankruptcy of the purchaser
When a purchaser is declared bankrupt in between sale and completion all of his or her property vests in the trustee in bankruptcy. The trustee can compel the vendor to complete the transaction by paying monies due by the allotted day. If the vendor wishes to proceed with the sale and the trustee is reluctant, the trustee has the right to claim that the contract is onerous. However, in these circumstances, the vendor can keep any deposit due to him.

Death of Vendor or purchaser

The personal representatives of a deceased vendor can compel the purchaser to sell. The money is conveyed to those representatives who will hold the money in accordance with the terms of any will or in accordance with the rules relating to intestacy if there is no will.

The same position applies to the purchaser's representatives, who can be compelled by the vendor to complete the purchase and who can hold money on the purchaser's behalf.

Now read the key points from chapter 7

Key Points From Chapter 7

- Conveyancing is about the practice of transferring a property from one to another.

- There are two main types of property ownership in Britain-Freehold and leasehold

- The lease is the single most important document if buying leasehold

- There are two systems of conveyancing – registered and unregistered.

- The contract of sale must be scrutinised thoroughly before exchange and completion

8

PLANNING MOVING ARRANGEMENTS

At this stage, you will either have sold your home and /or be ready to move into a new one. The process of moving home is closely linked with the completion of the purchase of another home. That is, assuming that you are moving to another bought property. Of course, you may be moving to a rented home.

However you choose to time your move, there are certain core tasks, as follows:

- Finalise removal and storage arrangements

- Contact electricity/gas/phone/cable companies and any other relevant company to tell them your moving date

- Organise your funds so that you can transfer all remaining money needed to complete the sale into your solicitors account for him/her to pay the sellers solicitor

One main question is: do you get a removal firm or do you do it yourself?

DIY moves

This is cheaper than hiring a removal company, especially if you have a few possessions or no big items of furniture. You will also need willing and able friends. However, do not take

the decision to move yourself lightly. Think carefully about the amount of furniture
that you have and the fact that your house may be a particularly difficult site to move from.

Using professionals

Professionals know what they are doing and can leave you to organise all the other aspects of moving whilst they do the donkeywork. This may cost you more money. However, it may be well worth it. Use a firm which is a member of the British Association of Removers (www.bar.co.uk). Members of this body have to adhere to a code of professional practice, meet minimum standards and provide emergency service and finance guarantees.

Removers can offer various levels of packing services. The most expensive option is for the remover to pack everything. The second most expensive option is for them to pack the breakable things such as glass. The cheapest way is for the removers to provide crates and for you to do your own packing.

If you are going for the professional option:

- Get two or three estimates. You can find the names of local firms through the British Association of Removers, through the yellow pages (www.yell.com) or through Thomson's Directories (www.thomweb.co.uk)

- There are a growing number of websites that include quotes from removal firms (see below)

- You should expect estimators to go through your whole property including gardens and loft

- Check whether your possessions will be covered by your household insurance policy and extend the cover of they are not
- Don't wait to exchange contracts to organise removers.

The following Websites may be useful:
www.reallymoving.com
This site was launched in 1999 and is the leading provider of online removal services. Registering on the site will get you three quotes from removers. It also covers solicitors, surveyors and others involved in the buying and selling process.

Contacting utilities

A boring but essential task is to contact all of the companies that provide you with services to tell them that you have moved. This should be done after you exchange contracts, obtaining meter readings etc. Most utilities will ask you for confirmation of your new address and moving date in writing. If you cannot face this task then use the following website:

www.ihavemoved.com

This site was started in 1999 by a consortium of investors and industry figures. The claim is to be the UK's first free online change of address service. You register, enter your old and new address, supply account numbers and meter readings where relevant and ihavemoved will send the information to the appropriate companies. The process is quick and relatively uncomplicated.

www.simplymove.co.uk
This site offers a similar service

9

BUYING AND SELLING IN SCOTLAND

Scotland has it own system of law, and buying and selling a house or flat is quite a different process from doing so in England, Wales or Northern Ireland.

The system generally works more quickly and there is less risk of gazumping.

Looking for property

Solicitors, property centres and offices. These are the largest source of properties available in Scotland. Often found in town centres, the property centres provide information in a similar way to estate agents outside Scotland.

Newspapers. Daily Scottish newspapers are a good source of property. Regional and local newspapers carry many details on a regular basis.

Estate agents. These offer the same service

Ownership of property in Scotland

Property in Scotland does not exist as freehold or leasehold, as in England. Instead a "feudal tenure" system exists. This means that, as in freehold, the owner has right to building and land. However, the original owner of the development still has some say over any alterations and use of the land.

101

These feuing conditions are permanent and should be checked before purchase is considered. A new owner (feuar) can negotiate to have conditions waived, but there may be a charge for this. Further details of the system can be obtained from the lands tribunal for Scotland or your solicitor.

House prices

Property in Scotland is normally sold as "offers over" (sometimes called the upset price) the price set is usually the minimum and may not be negotiated down. This method is used where the property is likely to prove popular and to get the best price. If a quick sale is required a property may be sold as "fixed price" the seller will take the first offer at that price.

If there is more than one prospective purchaser the seller may opt to set a closing date for offers. The process is then like a blind bid, with none of the buyers knowing the price anyone else is bidding. Although the seller usually accepts the highest price, this is not always the case; other factors, such as date of entry, may be taken into consideration.

The buying process

Surveys

These are carried out before a formal offer is made. In some circumstances you may end up losing money, if your offer is not accepted. There are no licensed conveyancers in Scotland. Because solicitors do all the conveyancing and are so involved in the process then they will usually arrange surveys.

Making an offer

Your interest in buying a house is relayed via your solicitor to the selling solicitor by word of mouth. It does not have any legal standing and either party may pull out. Formal offer comes by letter, through the solicitor, and will include any items such as fixtures and fittings. The letter forms part of contract of sale.

Exchange of missives

If the offer is accepted, a formal letter called qualified acceptance is returned by the sellers solicitor, confirming or amending the conditions. The entry date may need to be negotiated to suit both parties. These formal letters are referred to as missives and may go back and forth for clarification.

Missives concluded

Once all the conditions are agreed, the purchase is then legally binding for both buyer and seller. The missives are concluded by the acting solicitors: neither the buyer or the seller signs anything. There is no deposit paid in the Scottish system except if you are buying a new house from a property developer

The law states that once the missives have been concluded, the purchaser is responsible for the insurance of the property. However, it is more usual for an agreement to be made in the missives that the seller remains liable until the date of entry.

The date that you would like to move is suggested in your formal offer to the seller. In this time you should be able to sell your house and complete any legal work. Before the date of entry, your solicitor will prepare what is known as a disposition to confirm the change of ownership. He will obtain from the sellers solicitor the title deeds which will be signed by the seller to agree the change of ownership. These will be handed over on the date of entry following payment of the property price.

Searches

There are two types of searches in Scotland:

Immediately prior to exchanging missives a search on the property and against the individual is made. This checks that the seller has a good title to the property and that the purchaser can grant security for the loan;

A local authority search forms part of the missives. It checks that there are no proposed developments that would affect the property.

Selling a house or flat

Ways of selling your home

The majority of houses are bought and sold through solicitor offices, but you also have the options of selling through an estate agent or selling it privately yourself. Whatever option you choose, it is customary in Scotland to show prospective buyers around the house and explain the details.

DIY selling

This involves setting the price, preparing the sales details about the house, advertising it and showing people around. The advantages of this kind of sale are that you cut out middlemen and save commission. However, you will need a solicitor for conveyancing.

Selling through an estate agent

These are normally Scottish branches of well-known chains of agents. They offer a service similar to their English counterparts. In contrast to selling through a solicitor, estate agents often encourage you to take the first offer rather than generating interest and setting a closing date. You should get quotes from agents about their charges. this will be typically around 1.5% of selling price.

Selling through a solicitor

Most property in Scotland is sold through solicitors. They provide a service similar to estate agents and have property centres displaying details of houses for sale, although there may be an extra one off charge for this depending on the area you are in. Their commission charges are often slightly cheaper than those of estate agents. It is normal practice to use the same solicitor to sell your house and carry out the legal side of the sale.

The selling process

Your solicitor or estate agent will prepare the sales particulars and discuss the selling price with you as part of their contract. Depending upon the circumstances, they will advise as to whether the house is sold as "offers above" or as "fixed price". The former is usually set slightly below the expected price to encourage buyers. If a degree of competitiveness is created you may be able to set a "closing" date which usually achieves a better selling price.

Legally you should leave all fixtures and fittings, such as carpets and curtains or kitchen equipment unless you draw up a contract which states otherwise.

The legal services of your solicitor

There are two main areas the solicitor will need to follow up to allow smooth progress of a house sale.

The title deeds will need to be examined to check that you are the true owner of the property. Scottish law includes the Matrimonial Homes (Family Protection) (Scotland) Act: even if only one spouse owns the property permission to sell must be given by the partner.

Conveyancing will involve property surveys, and local searches to check there are no proposals for developments.

If you are using a solicitor to sell your house, they may offer an overall charge that covers selling and legal services.

Accepting offers

Your solicitor will inform you if anyone has shown an interest in your property. If a lot of interest is shown in your house, you could consider setting a closing date for offers. Your solicitor or estate agent should advise you whether this is a good idea. There is no point in setting a date until you are sure more than one person is likely to make a formal offer.

The closing date is a specific time on a specific day that all formal offers will be assessed. You are not obliged to accept any offer if they are too low. Nor does the highest offer have to be accepted.

If you accept the highest offer, your solicitor may negotiate points concerning other conditions, such as extras included or dates, but there must be no attempt to try to raise the price offered. If you are using an estate agent, their role ends once the offer has been handed over to the solicitor.

A formal offer will include all the conditions of sale, the price, any items included, and the date of entry. Some offers are made with a time limit in which you must accept verbally, which can be as little as within 24 hours. You should seek advice from your solicitors whether to act promptly. You may be advised to hold out for a higher offer. If the purchaser is seriously interested they will not mind waiting for an acceptance.

Your solicitor will engage in the process of exchanging missives with the buyers solicitor. Missives are formal letters laying down conditions of sale and may be passed back and forth until an amicable agreement is reached. Once final missives have been exchanged the contract is legally binding for both parties, so it is important that you are familiar with all the conditions being negotiated by your solicitor through the missives. It will be too late once they have finally been changed.

Setting an entry date

The date for finalising the sale is suggested by both the seller and by the buyer in his offer. It is negotiated by both parties, and a mutually agreed date is written into the missives. This is the date when the keys are handed to your solicitor, and you must move out. although the date of entry is set by the seller it may need to be changed to achieve a compromise which suits you and the purchaser.

Completion

Title deeds. Your buyers solicitor will need to prepare the disposition and for this your solicitor will send the title deeds. The disposition is the document that states the change of ownership on the title deeds, and will need to be signed by you. It is handed over to the purchasers solicitor in exchange for payment of the property on the date of settlement.

Now read the Key Points from Chapter eight overleaf.

Key Points From Chapter 8

- The process of buying and selling property in Scotland is quite different to that in England.

- Property in Scotland does not exist as freehold or leasehold. Instead a Feudal tenure exists.

- "Gazumping" is not possible in Scotland. Once an offer is made it is virtually binding.

- Solicitors play a very important part in the process of buying and selling property in Scotland.

9

BUYING OVERSEAS

Thousands of Britons have purchased properties overseas. However, this can be problematic and certainly basic advice is needed relating to the particular country where you are buying. There are a few general tips when buying abroad:

- Buy through a qualified and licensed agent. In most countries including France, Spain, Portugal and the USA, agents legally have to be licensed and using an unlicensed agent means that there is no comeback if things go wrong.

- Do not sign anything until you are sure that you understand it. Note that estate agents in the above countries will tend to do more of the legal work than in Britain and hence charge more commission.

- Always hire a solicitor (English speaking if you are not fluent in the local language) to act for you. In some countries, the locals do not use solicitors but you should insist. The solicitor will check that the seller owns the property and that there are no debts attached to it and that planning regulations have been met. Local searches are not as regulated as they are in the UK and it's often a case of making informal enquiries at the local town hall.

- Understand the role played by the state notary (notaire in France, notario in Spain) he or she is a state official, whose only role is to see that the sale is completed. He or she will not act for you or the seller.

There are a few useful websites where more information can be gained:

www.french-property-news.com

This site is the online arm of the magazine French property News. It claims to have the most comprehensive list of properties on the web and also has details of other organisations.

www.french-property.com

Similar to the above

www.europropertynet.com

This is a European wide estate agency service, carrying a wide range of properties from around Europe, including France, Spain, Portugal and Greece. Other advice is also available on this site.

For property in Spain, try www.spanishpropertyco.co.uk which specialises in retirement property. For general tips on buying in Spain go to www.cornishco.com a firm of UK lawyers specialising in Spanish property.

Glossary of Terms

Arrangement fee-Sum payable to secure a fixed rate, capped rate or discount mortgage offer.

Asking price-The price set by the seller and his/her agent for a property, It is common for offers to be above the asking price in rising markets and below in falling markets.

Bargain (Scotland)-When an offer on a property has been accepted. The bargain is made at the conclusion of missives.

Bridging loan-Loans advanced when a homeowner has bought a property but has not yet sold his/her current home.

Buyers market-When the market is falling, sellers are desperate to offload property and will take low prices.

Capped rate- Mortgage rate which can only rise up to a set ceiling or cap for a set number of years but which falls if the base rate rises.

Cashback-Cash sum paid to borrowers by lenders as part of certain mortgage deals as incentive.

Chain-A series of transactions depending on each other to go through, as sellers need to sell their property in order to buy another.

Collective enfranchisement-the process of clubbing together with other leaseholders in a block of leasehold flats and buying the freehold of the block.

Completion date-The date when the property changes hands, the balance of the purchase price is handed over and keys given to new owner.

Conclusion of missives (Scotland)-The point at which the property sale becomes binding and a bargain is made.

Conveyancing-The legal process of transferring ownership of land and property from one individual or company to another.

Deposit-Sum payable at exchange of contracts.

Downvaluing-The valuation put on the property by the lenders surveyor is lower than the price the buyer is prepared to pay.

Draft contract-Early version of contract drawn up by the sellers solicitor.

Endowment-Savings/insurance policy often linked to an interest only mortgage to build up money to pay off the loan at the end. Have been discredited of late.

Exchange of contracts-The stage in the housebuying process in England and Wales at which a deal becomes binding.

Fixed rate-A mortgage rate that is fixed for a set period, usually tow, three or five years.

Flexible mortgage-A loan which allows over or under payment and which can be set against a current account to reduce the overall outstanding debt.

Freehold-Outright ownership of a property and the land on which it stands.

Gazumping-A seller accepts a firm offer for a property, then drops the buyer in favour of another offering a higher price.

Gazundering-A buyer makes a firm offer then threatens to pull out unless the seller accepts a lower price.

Ground rent-A small annual payment payable by leaseholdersn to freeholders

Homebuyers report-A type of property survey less detailed than a full structural survey but more detailed than a valuation survey.

Interest only mortgage-Monthly repayments are made up of interest only with the final capital sum payable at the end.

Joint sole agency-Two agents market the same property.

Leasehold-Occupation of a property for a certain number of years. Typically a buyer will purchase a lease with a certain number of years left and it is important to check the lease is not too short for mortgage and resale purposes.

Loan to value-the proportion of a property's value borrowed as a mortgage.

Local search-Information sought from local authorities by the buyers solicitor during the housebuying process.

Mortgage indemnity guarantee-Extra premium levied by mortgage brokers on borrowers needing a large proportion of the property's value, normally over 90%.

Mortgage payment protection insurance-Covers mortgage payments in the event of accident, sickness or unemployment.

Multiple agency-The property is marketed by several agents and whichever sells the property gets the commission.

Negative equity-A mortgage secured on the property is higher than the property's value. Happens when house prices fall sharply.

Offer-The process of deciding to buy a property and naming your price.

Offplan-The process of buying a new property from floorplans. This can be the aski9ng price or a lower or higher price.

Part exchange-a developer takes your current home and sells it on for you so you can buy a new built home.

Redemption penalty-Sum payable on certain mortgage deals for cashing in the loan before the end of a set period.

Repayment mortgage-Loan repayments are a mixture of capital and interest and the mortgage is guaranteed to be paid off at the end of the term.

Secured loan-Mortgage or other loan backed by property allowing the lender to repossess the property if payments are not made.

Self-certification loan-Mortgage granted without need for proof of income.

Seller's market-When demand for property is high and buyers are willing to pay top prices.

Sellers pack-A government proposal to speed up the housebuying process by requiring sellers to put together a pack of information on their properties before marketing them. Introduced on a pilot basis with full implementation July 2007.

Service Charges-Charges levied on tenants of leasehold properties for repairs maintenance and general upkeep. Normally paid annually but may be extra demands if additional work needed.

Sinking fund-A fund built up by leaseholders for future major repairs to a building.

Sole agency-A single estate agent acting on a seller's behalf.

Stamp duty-A government tax levied on the purchase of all properties changing hands for more than £60,000. The tax is banded with properties bought for between £60,001 and £250,000 charged at 1% of purchase price, properties between £250,001 and £500,000 3% and above £500,000 4%.

Standard variable rate-The standard mortgage rate. Moves up and down with base rates.

Structural survey-A detailed survey of the condition of a property. The most expensive type of survey available to homebuyers.

Title deeds-legal documents setting out the ownership of a property.

Valuation-The process of putting a price on a property. Used by estate agents and professional valuers in determining the value of a property.

10

A SUMMARY OF USEFUL WEBSITES

Buying property.

Local government and local area sites.

The Local Government Association www.lganet.gov.uk
Confederation of Scottish Local Authorities www.cosla.gov.uk
Greater London Authority www.london.gov.uk
www.upmystreet.com
www.yell.com
www.homecheckuk.com
www.streetmap.co.uk

House prices

Halifax www.halifax.co.uk
Nationwide www.nationwide.co.uk
Land Registry www.landreg.gov.uk

Property search sites

www.reapit.com for reviews of property websites

Buying agents
Knight Frank www.knightfrank.com
FPD Savills www.fpdsavills.co.uk

Selling property

The National Association of Estate Agents www.naes.org.uk
The Royal Institution of Chartered Surveyors www.rics.org.uk
The Estate Agents Ombudsman Scheme www.oea.co.uk

Property search sites

www.hometrack.co.uk
www.rightmove.co.uk
www.assertahome.co.uk
www.fish4.co.uk
www.propertyfinder.co.uk
www.primelocation.com
www.findaproperty.com
www.08004homes.co.uk
www.thisislondon.co.uk

House Doctor

www.thefinaltouch.co.uk

Leasehold/freehold advice

Lease www.lease-advice.org
Association of Residential Managing Agents www.arma.org.uk

Moving costs www.woolwich.co.uk

Finances

Financial services Authority www.fsa.gov.uk
Mortgage Code Compliance Board www.mortgagecode.org.uk
Financial Ombudsman Service www.financial-ombudsman.org.uk
Association of British Insurers www.abi.org.uk

Online mortgage sites/brokers

Moneyfacts www.moneyfacts.co.uk
www.find.co.uk
www.moneysupermarket.co.uk
www.moneynet.co.uk
www.moneyextra.com

New Homes

National Association of new Homeowners www.nanho.org.uk
NHBC www.nhbc.co.uk

New homes property search

www.freeagents.co.uk
www.newhomesnetwork.co.uk

Self Build

www.homebuilding.co.uk
www.plotfinder.net
www.buildstore.co.uk
www.ebuild.co.uk

Removals

The British Association of Removers www.bar.co.uk
www.reallymoving.com
www.ihavemoved.com
www.simplymove.co.uk

House swapping

www.webswappers.com

Auctions www.propwatch.com

Overseas agents

Hamptons International www.hamptons.co.uk
Knight Frank www.knightfrank.com
FPD Savills www.fpdsavills.co.uk

Overseas property search sites

www.french-property-news.com
www.french-property.com
www.europropertynet.com
www.spanishproperty.com
www.cornishco.com

If you have any comments about this book or would like to contact Straightforward Publishing please e mail info@straightforwardco.co.uk or write to:

Straightforward Publishing 106 Ladysmith Road Brighton BN2 4EG.

www.straightforwardco.co.uk

All titles, listed below, in the Straightforward Guides Series can be purchased online, using credit card or other forms of payment by going to www.straightfowardco.co.uk A discount of 25% per title is offered with online purchases.

Law
A Straightforward Guide to:

Competition Law
Consumer Rights
Bankruptcy Insolvency and the Law
Employment Law
Private Tenants Rights
Family law
Small Claims in the County Court
Contract law
Intellectual Property and the law
Debt Advice
Divorce and the law
Leaseholders Rights
The Process of Conveyancing
Knowing Your Rights and Using the Courts
Producing Your own Will
Housing Rights
The Bailiff the law and You
Probate and The Law
Company law
What to Expect When You Go to Court
Guide to Competition Law
Give me Your Money-Guide to Effective Debt Collection
Caring for a Disabled Child

General titles

Letting Property for Profit
Buying, Selling and Renting property
Buying a Home in England and France
Bookkeeping and Accounts for Small Business

Creative Writing
Freelance Writing
Writing Your own Life Story
Writing performance Poetry
Writing Romantic Fiction
Speech Writing

Teaching Your Child to Read and write
Teaching Your Child to Swim
Raising a Child-The Early Years

Creating a Successful Commercial Website
The Straightforward Business Plan
The Straightforward C.V.
Successful Public Speaking

Handling Bereavement
Play the Game-A Compendium of Rules
Individual and Personal Finance
Understanding Mental Illness
The Two Minute Message
Guide to Self Defence
Buying a Used Car
Tiling for Beginners
Go to:
www.straightforwardco.co.uk